Sharing with Others

An introduction to financial literacy

by Mattie Reynolds

RED
CHAIR
•PRESS•

Please visit our website at **www.redchairpress.com**.

Find a free catalog of all our high-quality products for young readers.

Sharing with Others

Publisher's Cataloging-In-Publication Data
(Prepared by The Donohue Group, Inc.)

Reynolds, Mattie.
Sharing with others : an introduction to financial literacy / by Mattie Reynolds.
p. : col. ill. ; cm. -- (Start smart: money)
Issued also as an ebook.
Summary: Learn how sharing your time, goods, and money can help those in need. This book will teach you words and ideas about sharing.
Interest age group: 004-008.
Includes bibliographical references and index.
ISBN: 978-1-937529-44-4 (hardcover)
ISBN: 978-1-937529-40-6 (pbk.)
1. Sharing--Juvenile literature. 2. Children--Finance, Personal--Juvenile literature. 3. Sharing. 4. Finance, Personal. I. Title.
BJ1533.G4 R49 2013

179/.9   2012943326

Photo credits:
Copyright Girl Scouts of the USA. All Rights Reserved: pages 16-17
Dreamstime: pages 15, 18, 19, 20, back cover
iStockphoto LP: pages front cover, 1, 5, 7, 8, 11, 12, 13, 21
Shutterstock Images LLC: pages 3, 4, 6, 9, 10, 14

Reading specialist: Linda Cornwell, Literacy Connections Consulting

This edition first published in 2013 by

Red Chair Press LLC   PO Box 333   South Egremont, MA 01258-0333

Printed in The United States of America

1 2 3 4 5 17 16 15 14 13

Table of Contents

Words in **bold type** are defined in the glossary.

CHAPTER 1

All People Have Needs

Do you like going to the movies? Maybe you have your heart set on getting a new toy you saw on television. These are things you want but you do not need them. Think about things you need.

We all have basic needs such as food, clothes, and a place to live. Every person needs clothes. But you do not need fancy new clothes. You need food. But you do not need an **expensive** new cereal.

Food, clothes and shelter are basic needs.

Everyone has to eat to be healthy and have energy. Adults **earn** money by working at a job. One of the most important ways the adult uses money is to buy food for their family.

People need clothes, too. Clothes help keep
you warm in the winter and cool in the summer.
Some kids get new clothes when school starts.
Some kids get to wear the clothes their older
brother or sister wore.

Everyone needs a place to live. Some
people live in a house. Others live in
apartment buildings where many people live.
Where you live provides **shelter** from the
weather and keeps you and your family safe.

Who pays for the food, clothes, and place to live? Usually an adult in the family has a job to earn money for these things. But not everyone earns enough money to pay for all three basic needs.

CHAPTER 2

Donation box

Sharing Goods and Money

Money helps us buy the things we need. But some things cost a lot of money. Some people need help to provide things their family needs. They may go to a place in their community for help. There are many ways we can help, too.

Food banks collect boxes and cans of food. Then people can get the food for free or at a low cost. Some people buy an extra can of vegetables or box of cereal to **donate** to food banks. The food is then shared with families who need it.

Some people share goods with others.

Micheala is growing fast. She cannot wear some of her clothes now. She and her mom collected clothes from their family to donate to a clothing drive. Micheala will miss some of her favorite things. But she knows another girl will enjoy the clothes as much as she did!

Jonah has a job walking dogs in his neighborhood. He earns $5 each week. Jonah likes to save some of his money. But every week he puts $1 into a special jar for **charity**. Now Jonah shares his money with the local animal shelter. Pets have needs too!

CHAPTER 3

Giving to Others

Some kids don't have jobs. That does not mean they can't help others. How can kids help people where they live if they do not earn money? There are many ways and they won't cost a penny.

Kids can give back to their community and help others by volunteering their time. Some kids have great ideas, too. They work with their scouting and other groups to come up with ideas for helping.

Sharing time helps you
and others feel good.

Maya belongs to a group of girls that meets
every week. The girls talked together to come
up with ways they could help others. The group
set a goal to collect used eyeglasses for one
month to give to a local charity.

They decorated boxes and took the boxes
to school, to churches, and to local businesses.
They even stood outside the supermarket with
an adult leader every Saturday. After one month,
the glasses they collected really piled up!

Micah does not earn money. But he likes to talk
– a lot! His neighbor, Mr. Tanaka, does not have
family or friends near by. Two days each week,
Micah spends an hour with his neighbor. They
talk about what Micah is learning and what he
has done that week.

Some days Micah and his sister play games with Mr. Tanaka. They talk about all the things Mr. Tanaka remembers when he was their age, too. They all love that part!

It feels good to earn money. Money lets
us buy things we need and things we want.
But spending money isn't the only reason to
earn. Sharing our goods, time, and money
with people who need help not only makes us
feel good, it makes someone else feel good, too.

Glossary

charity: an organization that provides help and raises money for people in need

donate: give something like goods or services for a good cause

earn: to get paid money in return for labor or services

expensive: costing a lot of money

shelter: a place that gives protection from bad weather and danger

For More Information

Books

Lewis, Barbara A. *The Kid's Guide to Service Projects*. Minneapolis, MN: Free Spirit, 2009.

Otfinoski, Steve. *The Kid's Guide to Money: Earning It, Saving It, Spending It, Growing It, Sharing It*. New York, NY: Scholastic, 1995.

Sabin, Ellen. *The Giving Book*. New York, NY: Watering Can Press, 2004

Web Sites

Learning to Give
http://www.learningtogive.org/students/

TheMint.org: Helping Others
http://www.themint.org/kids/giving.html

Note to educators and parents: Our editors have carefully reviewed these web sites to ensure they are suitable for children. Web sites change frequently, however, and we cannot guarantee that a site's future contents will continue to meet our high standards of quality and educational value. You may wish to preview these sites and closely supervise children whenever they access the Internet.

Index

About the Author

Mattie Reynolds practices the four basic skills of financial literacy in her life. She earned money in the insurance business and learned to save for things her family needed. Mattie continues to be a smart shopper buying what she needs and saving for what she wants. She shares with her church and charity in Duncan, Oklahoma, where she lives.